MARYLAND

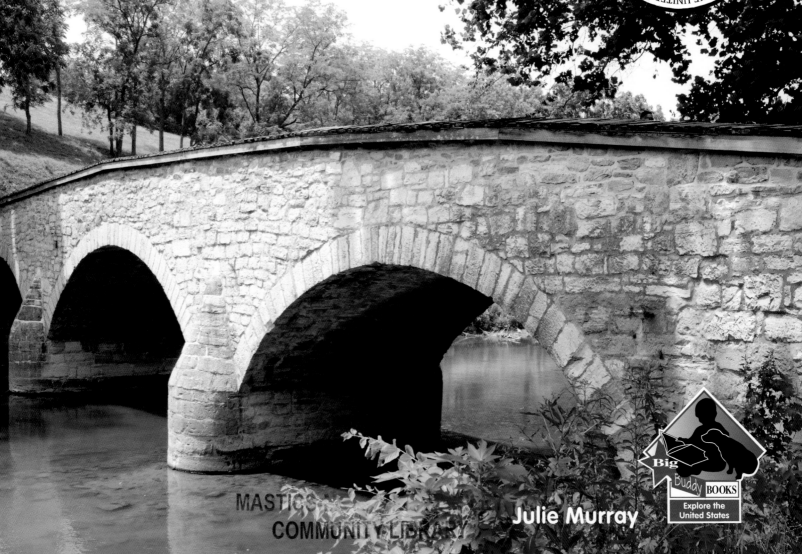

Julie Murray

Big Buddy BOOKS
Explore the
United States

VISIT US AT
www.abdopublishing.com

Published by ABDO Publishing Company, PO Box 398166, Minneapolis, MN 55439.

Printed in the United States of America, North Mankato, Minnesota.
042012
092012

 PRINTED ON RECYCLED PAPER

Coordinating Series Editor: Rochelle Baltzer
Editor: Sarah Tieck
Contributing Editors: Megan M. Gunderson, BreAnn Rumsch, Marcia Zappa
Graphic Design: Adam Craven
Cover Photograph: *Shutterstock*: Jeffrey M. Frank.
Interior Photographs/Illustrations: *AP Photo*: The Baltimore Sun, Barbara Haddock Taylor (p. 25), Nick Ut
   (p. 25); *CORBIS*: ©Bettmann (p. 23); *Getty Images*: Walter Bibikow/The Image Bank (p. 11), Dennis Drenner
   (p. 26), MPI (p. 13), Jack Rosen/Photo Researchers (p. 30); *Glow Images*: Rob Crandall (p. 19); *iStockphoto*:
   ©iStockphoto.com/BackyardProduction (p. 17), ©iStockphoto.com/Joesboy (p. 27), ©iStockphoto.com/rmarnold
   (p. 30), ©iStockphoto.com/WilliamSherman (pp. 21, 29); *Shutterstock*: 4736202690 (p. 26), Antenna International
   (p. 30), Lonnie Gorsline (p. 30), C. Kurt Holter (p. 27), JeninVA (p. 27), Lone Wolf Photos (p. 5), Dave Newman
   (p. 9), Henry E Stamm IV (p. 9).

All population figures taken from the 2010 US census.

Library of Congress Cataloging-in-Publication Data

Murray, Julie, 1969-
 Maryland / Julie Murray.
    p. cm. -- (Explore the United States)
 ISBN 978-1-61783-358-8
 1. Maryland--Juvenile literature. I. Title.
 F181.3.M875 2013
 975.2--dc23
                    2012005984

MARYLAND

Contents

One Nation

The United States is a **diverse** country. It has farmland, cities, coasts, and mountains. Its people come from many different backgrounds. And, its history covers more than 200 years.

Today the country includes 50 states. Maryland is one of these states. Let's learn more about Maryland and its story!

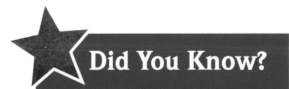

Did You Know?

Maryland became a state on April 28, 1788. It was the seventh state to join the nation.

4

Chesapeake Bay has shaped Maryland. It cuts deep into the state's land.

MARYLAND UP CLOSE

The United States has four main **regions**. Maryland is in the South.

Maryland shares borders with four states. Pennsylvania is north. Virginia and West Virginia are south and west. Delaware is east. The Atlantic Ocean is also east.

Maryland's total area is 10,441 square miles (27,042 sq km). About 5.8 million people live in the state.

REGIONS OF THE UNITED STATES

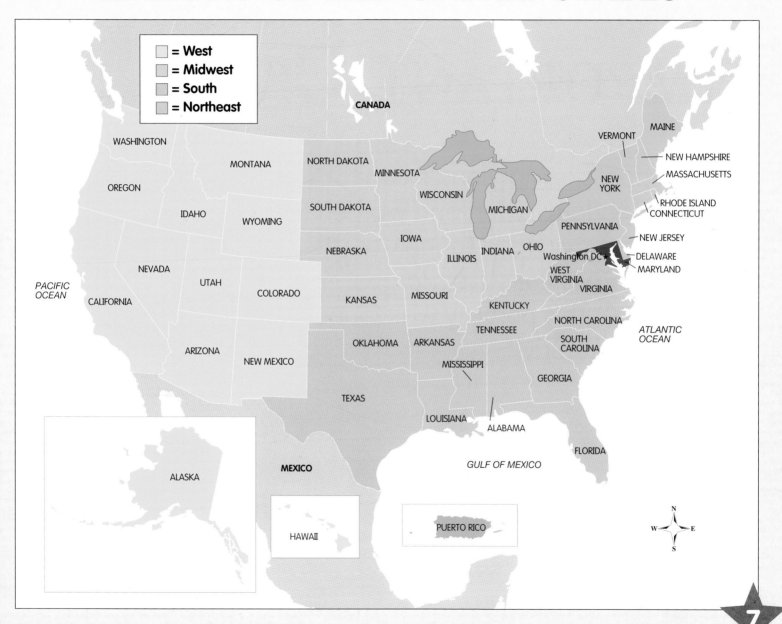

= West
= Midwest
= South
= Northeast

CANADA

WASHINGTON
MONTANA
NORTH DAKOTA
MINNESOTA
OREGON
IDAHO
WYOMING
SOUTH DAKOTA
WISCONSIN
MICHIGAN
NEW YORK
VERMONT
MAINE
NEW HAMPSHIRE
MASSACHUSETTS
RHODE ISLAND
CONNECTICUT
PENNSYLVANIA
NEW JERSEY
IOWA
NEBRASKA
ILLINOIS
INDIANA
OHIO
Washington DC
DELAWARE
MARYLAND
WEST VIRGINIA
VIRGINIA
NEVADA
UTAH
COLORADO
KANSAS
MISSOURI
KENTUCKY
CALIFORNIA
PACIFIC OCEAN
NORTH CAROLINA
TENNESSEE
SOUTH CAROLINA
ATLANTIC OCEAN
ARIZONA
NEW MEXICO
OKLAHOMA
ARKANSAS
MISSISSIPPI
GEORGIA
TEXAS
LOUISIANA
ALABAMA
FLORIDA
GULF OF MEXICO
ALASKA
MEXICO
HAWAII
PUERTO RICO

N
W   E
S

7

IMPORTANT CITIES

Annapolis is Maryland's **capital**. It is home to the US Naval Academy. Men and women train there to be part of the US Navy and Marine Corps.

Baltimore is the state's largest city. Its population is 620,961. This port city was founded in 1729 near Chesapeake Bay.

Did You Know?

Annapolis was the US capital from 1783 to 1784.

Maryland's State House is the oldest capitol building still in use. And, it is the only one that has also been the US capitol!

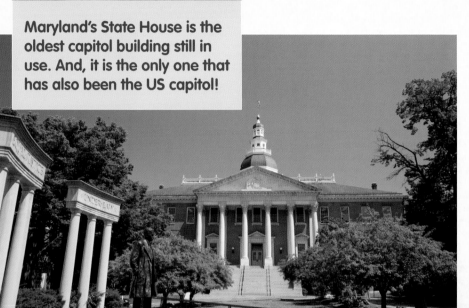

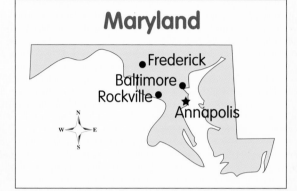

Maryland

Frederick
Baltimore
Rockville
Annapolis

N W E S

Baltimore's popular waterfront area is called the Inner Harbor. It has shops, restaurants, and hotels.

Frederick is Maryland's second-largest city, with 65,239 people. Today, many artists live there. During the **American Civil War**, major battles took place near Frederick. This city had hospitals for soldiers.

Rockville is the state's third-largest city. It is home to 61,209 people. Many people who live there work in nearby Washington DC.

Frederick is known for its skyline. It is called "the City of Clustered Spires."

11

MARYLAND IN HISTORY

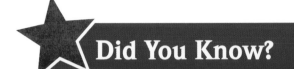

Did You Know?

Native Americans lived in Maryland for thousands of years before the American colonies formed.

Maryland's history includes wars and the start of the United States. In 1632, Maryland began as an English colony. In the 1700s, American colonists wanted to be part of a new country. So, they fought in the **Revolutionary War** and formed the United States. In 1788, Maryland became the seventh state.

Maryland's people were divided during the **American Civil War**. But, the state stayed part of the North. This helped guard the nearby US **capital**, Washington DC.

The Battle of Antietam took place in Maryland on September 17, 1862. About 23,000 civil war soldiers were hurt or killed. The battle stopped Southern soldiers from going north.

13

Timeline

1767

The Mason-Dixon Line set the border between Pennsylvania and Maryland. It is also considered the border between the northern and southern states.

1814

Francis Scott Key wrote "The Star-Spangled Banner" after witnessing a battle in Maryland.

1849

Harriet Tubman of Dorchester County escaped from **slavery**. She became famous for helping other slaves reach freedom.

1700s

1800s

Maryland became the seventh state on April 28.

1788

Maryland gave money and land to create the US **capital**, Washington DC.

1791

The **American Civil War** began. Maryland fought for the Northern states.

1861

14

1875

Ocean City's Atlantic Hotel opened. The surrounding beach became one of the East Coast's most popular beaches.

1942

President Franklin D. Roosevelt made land in Catoctin Mountain Park a special place for presidents to visit. Today, it is known as Camp David.

2010

An earthquake hit Maryland. Even though it was short and mild, it was the strongest in the area in 35 years.

1900s

2000s

A fire destroyed downtown Baltimore.

1904

Spiro T. Agnew of Baltimore became vice president of the United States. He served with President Richard Nixon.

1969

15

ACROSS THE LAND

Maryland has coasts, mountains, valleys, wetlands, and flat, open land. Many of its rivers empty into Chesapeake Bay. The Appalachian Mountains are in the western part of the state.

Many types of animals make their homes in Maryland. These include orioles, blue crabs, and oysters.

Did You Know?

In July, the average temperature in Maryland is 75°F (24°C). In January, it is 33°F (0.6°C).

Swallow Falls State Park is in the Appalachian Mountains. It is home to Maryland's highest waterfall, Muddy Creek Falls.

17

Earning a Living

Maryland is a service and manufacturing state. Several banking companies are based there. And with Washington DC nearby, many people work for the US government.

Many products are made in Maryland. These include food, drinks, and computer parts.

Did You Know?

Maryland farms produce milk, eggs, chicken, pork, and beef.

SPORTS PAGE

Many people think of sports when they think of Maryland. The state is home to two major sports teams. The Baltimore Ravens play football, and the Baltimore Orioles play baseball. And, Maryland hosts sailboat, horse, and car races.

People also enjoy outdoor activities in Maryland. They hunt, fish, and hike in the state's natural areas. And, they sail on Chesapeake Bay.

Skipjack races on Chesapeake Bay are popular sailing events.

HOMETOWN HEROES

Many famous people are from Maryland. Francis Scott Key was born in Frederick County in 1779. He is famous for writing "The Star-Spangled Banner."

During the **War of 1812**, Key watched a battle from a ship. He wrote about what he saw. Later, his words were set to music. In 1931, the song became the national **anthem** of the United States.

Key was excited to see the US flag flying above Fort McHenry after a British attack. So, he wrote a poem about it.

Michael Phelps was born in Baltimore in 1985. He is a famous swimmer. He has won races at the Summer Olympics and other important **championships**.

In 2008, Phelps won eight gold medals at the Summer Olympics. No one had ever won that many in one year! Some say Phelps is the best swimmer of all time.

In 2010, Phelps swam the butterfly and set a US record at the Maryland Swimming Championships.

Phelps trains with his coach, Bob Bowman, in Baltimore.

Tour Book

Do you want to go to Maryland? If you visit the state, here are some places to go and things to do!

 Cheer

Watch some steeplechasing! This type of horse racing is popular in Maryland. The Maryland Hunt Cup race is one of many that happen each spring.

 Taste

Try some blue crab. Fishermen catch this famous Maryland shellfish in Chesapeake Bay's salty waters.

 See

Visit the Assateague Island National Seashore. This island has about 300 wild ponies. No one knows for sure how they got there!

Remember

Walk the grounds where the Battle of Antietam took place near Sharpsburg.

Discover

Hike in Catoctin Mountain Park. People also camp, rock climb, and cross-country ski there.

A Great State

The story of Maryland is important to the United States. The people and places that make up this state offer something special to the country. Together with all the states, Maryland helps make the United States great.

The Appalachian Mountains are one of Maryland's natural wonders.

Fast Facts

Date of Statehood:
April 28, 1788

Population (rank):
5,773,552
(19th most-populated state)

Total Area (rank):
10,441 square miles
(42nd largest state)

Motto:
"Fatti Maschii, Parole Femine"
(Manly Deeds, Womanly
Words)

Nickname:
Free State, Old Line State

State Capital:
Annapolis

Flag:

Flower: Black-Eyed Susan

Postal Abbreviation:
MD

Tree: White Oak

Bird: Baltimore Oriole

Important Words

American Civil War the war between the Northern and Southern states from 1861 to 1865.

anthem a song of praise.

capital a city where government leaders meet.

championship a game, a match, or a race held to find a first-place winner.

diverse made up of things that are different from each other.

region a large part of a country that is different from other parts.

Revolutionary War a war fought between England and the North American colonies from 1775 to 1783.

slavery the practice of owning people as slaves. A slave is a person who is bought and sold as property.

War of 1812 a war between the United States and England from 1812 to 1815.

Web Sites

To learn more about Maryland, visit ABDO Publishing Company online. Web sites about Maryland are featured on our Book Links page. These links are routinely monitored and updated to provide the most current information available.

www.abdopublishing.com

Index